GOOD MORNING GRACE

A 31 Day Devotional

Trish Robinson

BEGINNING THE DAY IN A CONVERSATION WITH GRACE

Unless otherwise indicated, all Scripture quotations are taken from the Amplified® Bible (AMP). Copyright © 2015 by The Lockman Foundation. Used by permission. www.lockman.org*

Verses marked NASB are taken from the New American Standard Bible®, Copyright © 1960, 1971, 1977, 1995, 2020 by The Lockman Foundation. Used by permission. www.lockman.org*

Verses marked MSG are taken from The Message, Copyright © 1993, 2002, 2018 by Eugene H. Peterson. Used by permission of NavPress. All rights reserved. Represented by Tyndale House Publishers, a Division of Tyndale House Ministries.

Verses marked CEV are taken from the Contemporary English Version, Copyright © 1991, 1992, 1995 by American Bible Society. Used by permission.

Verses marked NKJV are taken from The Authorized (King James) Version, Rights in the Authorized Version in the United Kingdom are vested in the Crown's patentee, Cambridge University Press

Verses marked KJV are taken from the New King James Version®, Copyright © 1982 by Thomas Nelson. Used by permission. All rights reserved.

Verses marked CEB are taken from the Common English Bible®, Copyright © 2010, 2011 by Common English Bible. ™ Used by permission. All rights reserved worldwide.

Verses marked NLT are taken from Holy Bible, New Living Translation, Copyright © 1996, 2004, 2015 by Tyndale House Foundation. Used by permission of Tyndale House Publishers, Carol Stream, Illinois 60188. All rights reserved.

Cover By S. Henderson of CoCoFree Graphics & Design, Cleveland, OH

Editing by J. Williams and Q. Murphy

Good Morning Grace ™
Copyright © 2023 Trish Robinson
Published by CoCoFREE Publishing, Euclid, Ohio 44123

ISBN 979-8-9881592-30 (hardcover)
ISBN 979-8-9881592-6-1 (pbk)

All rights reserved. No part of this publication may be reproduced, stored in a retrieval system, or transmitted in any form or by any means – electronic, mechanical, digital, photocopying, recording or any other – except for brief quotation in printed reviews, without the prior written permission of the publishers.

Dedication

This book is dedicated to the ones who have helped me heal (especially those who didn't give up), reminding me to be kind to myself and give back to me the same measure I give to everyone else. To the ones who are on a healing journey and the reflection may be hard to face, this book is dedicated to you too.

I pray you find a safe space.

May grace meet you every morning.

Table of Contents

Introduction: Good Morning Grace	1
Day One	2
Day Two	5
Day Three	8
Day Four	11
Day Five	14
Day Six	17
Day Seven	20
Day Eight	23
Day Nine	26
Day Ten	29
Day Eleven	32
Day Twelve	35
Day Thirteen	38
Day Fourteen	41
Day Fifteen	44
Day Sixteen	47
Day Seventeen	50
Day Eighteen	53
Day Nineteen	56
Day Twenty	59
Day Twenty-One	62
Day Twenty-Two	65
Day Twenty-Three	68
Day Twenty-Four	71
Day Twenty-Five	74
Day Twenty-Six	77

Day Twenty-Seven	80
Day Twenty-Eight	83
Day Twenty-Nine	86
Day Thirty	89
Day Thirty-One	92
About the Author	95

Introduction

Good Morning Grace,

It's me again, back to share my expectations – the goals I have in mind for today and even a new declaration. Yesterday was everything, no matter what took place. I saw myself differently, as I entered your safe space. I can't remember if I said thank you for sticking by me and asking mercy to come along. You've handled me so carefully, even when I was wrong. When I walked out the door to start my day, I saw faith fill the sky, and watched the Sonshine wink at me as a sign to assure I'll be just fine.

There's a melody that seems to ring in my soul, though there is no music I can hear. The beat of my heart helps to keep the tempo and with every breath I can feel it. I can inhale deeply "girl you've got this," and as I exhale remember I don't have to do it all in my own strength. The rhythm of life has its own tune and carries its own cadence.

Watching you consistently show up for me even when I turn away, reinforces just how much He cares, and it's proven every day. So, thank you grace for being the gift I know I don't deserve. The prayers, songs and scriptures you've placed here, every written word. As we read through this book may our spirits begin to SOAR, may we come back to this place every day growing even more. So, until tomorrow comes I'll celebrate today and with the voice that's left in me I say, "Good Morning Grace."

Trish

Day 1

Scripture: "We don't have a priest who is out of touch with our reality. He's been through the weakness and testing, experienced it all – all but the sin. So, let's walk right up to Him and get what he is so ready to give. Take the mercy, accept the help." – Hebrews 4:15 MSG

Song: Jireh – Bethel Music ft. Naomi Raine & Cory Asbury

Prayer: Dear God, help me to receive the grace you give, so that I can move through the day, the week, and the year free. Free from doubt, worry, fear and unforgiveness. Let me place my issues at your feet knowing that none of them are beyond you and that your help is readily available. Amen

Declaration: My feelings are real and felt by the Father, His grace reaches me even there.

Practical Point: On several post it notes, or index cards write "Grace is a gift I choose to receive." Put those up in the areas you frequent the most as a reminder that grace is always available.

Time to SOAR (The Interactive Work)

See, Observe, Apply and Respond

This is your opportunity to walk through the scripture reading, settle in the song, meditate on the prayer, adopt the declaration and work out the practical point. Grace is understood better through experience, take a minute to record yours.

S_____

_____

_____

O_____

_____

_____

A_____

_____

_____

R_____

_____

_____

The Space of Grace

Here is where you can write more notes, doodle or draw, drop a tear or tag a friend. You can even add a new thing about where you want grace to be seen.

Day 2

Scripture: "And the peace of God [that peace which reassures the heart, that peace] which transcends all understanding, [that peace which] stands guard over your hearts and your minds in Christ Jesus [is yours]." – Philippians 4:7 AMP

Song: Peace – Danny Gokey

Prayer: Dear God, help me to know Your peace – the peace that proceeds, prepares and permeates the spaces in my life where the enemy would want my teeth set on edge and mind filled with worry. Lord let me remember that beyond what I see and understand you are God. Stretch my thoughts and stabilize my heart. For all is well in you. Amen

Declaration: Peace permeates the places I have yet to inhabit and those that I have passed through, God is with me.

Practical Point: Write an acrostic for the word PEACE that can help you set your attention and intentions daily. (See my example)
P – pray for understanding
E – embrace the response
A – accept the plan and necessary adjustments
C – choose to obey
E – expand my belief and enlarge my capacity

Time to SOAR (The Interactive Work)

See, Observe, Apply and Respond

This is your opportunity to walk through the scripture reading, settle in the song, meditate on the prayer, adopt the declaration and work out the practical point. Grace is understood better through experience, take a minute to record yours.

S_____

_____

_____

O_____

_____

_____

A_____

_____

_____

R_____

_____

_____

The Space of Grace

Here is where you can write more notes, doodle or draw, drop a tear or tag a friend. You can even add a new thing about where you want grace to be seen.

Day 3

Scripture: "I have it all planned out – plans to take care of you, not abandon you, plans to give you the future you hope for. When you call on me, when you come and pray to me, I'll listen. When you come looking for me, you'll find me. Yes, when you get serious about finding me and want it more than anything else, I'll make sure you won't be disappointed." – Jeremiah 29:11-13 MSG

Song: I'm Alive – Rich Tolbert Jr.

Prayer: Dear God, you have carefully and creatively created a plan for my life. Help me to live according to each and every one of them. Give me guidance to make a schedule that would not overwhelm me and allow me to obey you. Let my thoughts, actions and words align with everything written concerning me. There is more, and I will live to see it all come to pass. Amen

Declaration: Because He has plans for me, I'll set intentional goals to see them all come to pass with great expectation.

Practical Point: Look at and review your goals for the day, week and month (if you haven't created any do that before the week is out. If anything doesn't add to or establish a clear purpose for you, consider removing or adjusting it. Review, rewrite and reconcile those that remain with the Father if necessary and seek his response.

Time to SOAR (The Interactive Work)

See, Observe, Apply and Respond

This is your opportunity to walk through the scripture reading, settle in the song, meditate on the prayer, adopt the declaration and work out the practical point. Grace is understood better through experience, take a minute to record yours.

S_____

_____

_____

O_____

_____

_____

A_____

_____

_____

R_____

_____

_____

The Space of Grace

Here is where you can write more notes, doodle or draw, drop a tear or tag a friend. You can even add a new thing about where you want grace to be seen.

Day 4

Scripture: "I will cry to God Most High, Who accomplishes all things on my behalf [for he completes my purpose in His plan]." – Psalm 57:2 AMP

Song: Never Lost – All Nations Worship Assembly Atlanta

Prayer: Dear God, may I have the faith I need to find the grace that fights for me. That same grace covers me and leads me back to Your throne to finish what you started. May I find it and cling to it with all hope and trust. Amen

Declaration: It's bigger than me, so God have your way.

Practical Point: Look at and identify three (3) areas where you have seen grace, given grace or needed grace. As you look at them were you able to see the same God in each? What was the difference, if any?

Time to SOAR (The Interactive Work)

See, Observe, Apply and Respond

This is your opportunity to walk through the scripture reading, settle in the song, meditate on the prayer, adopt the declaration and work out the practical point. Grace is understood better through experience, take a minute to record yours.

S_____

_____

_____

O_____

_____

_____

A_____

_____

_____

R_____

_____

_____

The Space of Grace

Here is where you can write more notes, doodle or draw, drop a tear or tag a friend. You can even add a new thing about where you want grace to be seen.

Day 5

Scripture: "These little troubles are getting us ready for an eternal glory that will make all our troubles seem like nothing. Things that are seen don't last forever, but things that are not seen are eternal. This is why we keep our minds on the things that cannot be seen." – 2 Corinthians 4:17-18 CEV

Song: Carry Us Through – All Nations ft. Maranda Curtis

Prayer: Lord, help me to find my life suitable for suffering and my service during it a sign of just how great you are. Let the moments of trouble still display measures of triumph with each step I take. Fix my focus on eternity when I am tempted to complain, reminding me that this is not the end. Amen

Declaration: There's a grace on my life to get through this and even more grace to grow from it. My suffering won't cause me to settle in it.

Practical Point: Pick one (1) thing you need God's help to get through and periodically praise Him throughout the day and week as if it has already taken place.

Time to SOAR (The Interactive Work)

See, Observe, Apply and Respond

This is your opportunity to walk through the scripture reading, settle in the song, meditate on the prayer, adopt the declaration and work out the practical point. Grace is understood better through experience, take a minute to record yours.

S_____

_____

_____

O_____

_____

_____

A_____

_____

_____

R_____

_____

_____

The Space of Grace

Here is where you can write more notes, doodle or draw, drop a tear or tag a friend. You can even add a new thing about where you want grace to be seen.

Day 6

Scripture: "When my life was slipping away, I remembered God, and my prayer got through to you, made it all the way to your Holy Temple." – Jonah 2:7 MSG

Song: Lord You Are Good – Todd Galbreath

Prayer: Dear God, help me to come to myself and catch myself before I fall. Life always has a way to start life-ing at the most inopportune times and will attempt to cause my faith to slip, but this isn't new to you. So, whatever is beyond me, let me lay it before you in prayer, remembering it was all preplanned and works for my good. Amen

Declaration: I don't have to be super in anything but submitted in all things.

Practical Point: For twenty-four (24) hours try to keep track of where you lack trust and try to control things in your life. Keep a tally and record of those things. The places where you haven't been able to put your total trust in prayer place them before God, asking Him to help you hand over what isn't yours to handle.

Time to SOAR (The Interactive Work)

See, Observe, Apply and Respond

This is your opportunity to walk through the scripture reading, settle in the song, meditate on the prayer, adopt the declaration and work out the practical point. Grace is understood better through experience, take a minute to record yours.

S_____

_____

_____

O_____

_____

_____

A_____

_____

_____

R_____

_____

_____

The Space of Grace

Here is where you can write more notes, doodle or draw, drop a tear or tag a friend. You can even add a new thing about where you want grace to be seen.

Day 7

Scripture: "God blesses you when people mock you and persecute you and lie about you and say all sorts of evil things against you because you are my followers. Be happy about it! Be very glad! For a great reward awaits you in heaven." – Matthew 5:11-12a NLT

Song: He Knows My Name – Tasha Cobbs Leonard

Prayer: Father, bridle my tongue and take hold of my tender heart. Help me to respond well where others expect me to fail. Give me kind words to speak or silence to maintain. Help me to celebrate the fact that you know me by name. Remind me of who you are and what that's worth to me, help me to silence the noise coming from the enemy. Amen

Declaration: My response is my responsibility and His reflection.

Practical Point: Take the time today to pray for those who are ready to ruin your character, integrity and morals.

Time to SOAR (The Interactive Work)

See, Observe, Apply and Respond

This is your opportunity to walk through the scripture reading, settle in the song, meditate on the prayer, adopt the declaration and work out the practical point. Grace is understood better through experience, take a minute to record yours.

S_____

_____

_____

O_____

_____

_____

A_____

_____

_____

R_____

_____

_____

The Space of Grace

Here is where you can write more notes, doodle or draw, drop a tear or tag a friend. You can even add a new thing about where you want grace to be seen.

Day 8

Scripture: "I sought the Lord [on the authority of His word], and He answered me, and delivered me from all my fears." - Psalm 34:4 AMP

Song: Lord Deliver Me – Donald Lawrence ft Le'Andria Johnson

Prayer: Lord, where I have been has been safe but also stagnant, help me to shift from the subtlety of living to soaring in the submission, surrender and my sacrifice of obedience. Move me closer to purpose and promise, unafraid to leave people, places and things behind that don't get me closer to you. Amen

Declaration: I'm walking away from comfort, convenience and complacency to embrace destiny.

Practical Point: Revisit your why in life and ask for instructions on how to find your way back to it.

Time to SOAR (The Interactive Work)

See, Observe, Apply and Respond

This is your opportunity to walk through the scripture reading, settle in the song, meditate on the prayer, adopt the declaration and work out the practical point. Grace is understood better through experience, take a minute to record yours.

S_____

_____

_____

O_____

_____

_____

A_____

_____

_____

R_____

_____

_____

The Space of Grace

Here is where you can write more notes, doodle or draw, drop a tear or tag a friend. You can even add a new thing about where you want grace to be seen.

Day 9

Scripture: "…Then, even though it's against the law, I will go to the king; and if I am to die, then I will die." – Esther 4:16 CEB

Song: Nevertheless – GMWA ft Avis Graves

Prayer: God help me to do the difficult thing that You are calling me to. Let me leave the details to you and walk in the ordered steps that you have created for me. Give me grace to go into places and before people that I don't feel qualified to face as if I belong there. Why? Because wherever I go, you are with me and where you have called me you've prepared me for. May I obey in obscurity and uncertainty, allowing your perfect will to be performed on my behalf. I say yes God, I say yes. Amen

Declaration: I don't understand and may not agree, but I will obey.

Practical Point: Do the thing that God has called you to do that terrifies you the most. Remember he didn't give you a spirit of fear, return it to the sender.

Time to SOAR (The Interactive Work)

See, Observe, Apply and Respond

This is your opportunity to walk through the scripture reading, settle in the song, meditate on the prayer, adopt the declaration and work out the practical point. Grace is understood better through experience, take a minute to record yours.

S_____

_____

_____

O_____

_____

_____

A_____

_____

_____

R_____

_____

_____

The Space of Grace

Here is where you can write more notes, doodle or draw, drop a tear or tag a friend. You can even add a new thing about where you want grace to be seen.

Day 10

Scripture: "Let my whole being bless the LORD and never forget all his good deeds:" - Psalm 103:2 CEB

Song: Always Remember – Rev. James Moore

Prayer: Lord my prayer today is simple, may I always remember everything you have done as I wait in expectation for what you will do. May every good deed of Your mighty hands flood my memory when I become anxiously eager as I wait. Amen

Declaration: He is the same God, so if He did it then I am sure He is able to do it again.

Practical Point: Confess and repent where you forgot to wait because you had foresight, believing you already knew what to do. Use that as a shaping tool to produce patience in your life.

Time to SOAR (The Interactive Work)

See, Observe, Apply and Respond

This is your opportunity to walk through the scripture reading, settle in the song, meditate on the prayer, adopt the declaration and work out the practical point. Grace is understood better through experience, take a minute to record yours.

S_____

_____

_____

O_____

_____

_____

A_____

_____

_____

R_____

_____

_____

The Space of Grace

Here is where you can write more notes, doodle or draw, drop a tear or tag a friend. You can even add a new thing about where you want grace to be seen.

Day 11

Scripture: "It's who you are and the way you live that count before God. Your worship must engage your spirit in the pursuit of truth. That's the kind of people the Father is out looking for: those who are simply and honestly themselves before Him in their worship. God is sheer being Himself – Spirit. Those who worship Him must do it out of their very being, their spirits, their true selves in adoration." – John 4:23ᵇ-24 MSG

Song: My Worship is For Real – Bishop Larry Trotter & Sweet Holy Spirit

Prayer: God may you always find me with a praise on my lips and a heart full of worship. May worship be a lifestyle for me just like prayer. I pray that with every wave of my hand, bowing of my head and sound coming from mouth will draw you near to me, exclaiming that is my daughter/son and I will dwell with them. Amen

Declaration: My worship will welcome Him to sit with me.

Practical Point: This may be a little challenging (go ahead and smile), stop what you're doing and with no music sing the first line of worship that comes to your heart.

Time to SOAR (The Interactive Work)

See, Observe, Apply and Respond

This is your opportunity to walk through the scripture reading, settle in the song, meditate on the prayer, adopt the declaration and work out the practical point. Grace is understood better through experience, take a minute to record yours.

S_____

_____

_____

O_____

_____

_____

A_____

_____

_____

R_____

_____

_____

The Space of Grace

Here is where you can write more notes, doodle or draw, drop a tear or tag a friend. You can even add a new thing about where you want grace to be seen.

Day 12

Scripture: "As each one has received a special gift, employ it in serving one another as good stewards of the multifaceted grace of God." 1 Peter 4:10 NASB

Song: Lord I'm Available to You by Milton Brunson

Prayer: I pray that every part of me be submitted for Your use. May you have Your way in, through and over my life. God get the glory out of every good and perfect gift that you have placed in me. May the seeds you have sown produce a harvest I am unable to hide that people will know you in totality and truth. Amen

Declaration: I will leave this earth empty because I was used up for His glory. Everything that I am is at His disposal.

Practical Point: Draw up a list of your gifts and talents. Now identify how they are being used or could be. Talk to someone about the ones on the shelf or in the sand.

Time to SOAR (The Interactive Work)

See, Observe, Apply and Respond

This is your opportunity to walk through the reading, settle in the song, meditate on the prayer, adopt the declaration and work out the practical point. Grace is understood better through experience, take a minute to record yours.

S_____

_____

_____

O_____

_____

_____

A_____

_____

_____

R_____

_____

_____

The Space of Grace

Here is where you can write more notes, doodle or draw, drop a tear or tag a friend. You can even add a new thing about where you want grace to be seen.

Day 13

Scripture: "None of this fazes us because Jesus loves us. I am absolutely convinced that nothing – nothing living or dead, angelic or demonic, today or tomorrow, high or low, thinkable or unthinkable – absolutely nothing can get between us and God's love because of the way that Jesus our Master has embraced us." – Romans 8:38-39 MSG

Song: Reckless Love by Cory Asbury

Prayer: God thank you for finding me worth the sacrifice and pursuit of both life and death on my behalf. May I always remember when life takes me low, that you'll come for me. And it until I am safe back in your care and wings, I pray hell be reminded it can't have me because I am yours and you will tear down everything in your way until you get me back.

Declaration: To Him I was worth the sacrifice.

Practical Point: Talk to someone who you know is not saved and share the love of Christ with them. Let them know how far he will go (your testimony) to get his child back.

Time to SOAR (The Interactive Work)

See, Observe, Apply and Respond

This is your opportunity to walk through the scripture reading, settle in the song, meditate on the prayer, adopt the declaration and work out the practical point. Grace is understood better through experience, take a minute to record yours.

S_____

_____

_____

O_____

_____

_____

A_____

_____

_____

R_____

_____

_____

The Space of Grace

Here is where you can write more notes, doodle or draw, drop a tear or tag a friend. You can even add a new thing about where you want grace to be seen.

Day 14

Scripture: "The Lord said to Abram, "Leave your land, your family, and your father's household for the land I will show you." "Abram left just as the Lord told him..." – Genesis 12:1, 4 CEB

Song: Oceans – Hillsong

Prayer: Heaven, guide me with God holding my hand into the unknown. Settle my fear and secure my faith. God speak to the winds as I walk and move the mountain as I climb. Take me up and over every obstacle, barrier and detour that wasn't designed by You. Beckon me to come and let me waste no time in my response. Amen

Declaration: Fear won't keep where I'm called to leave or force me from where I am called to stay.

Practical Point: Look over and examine your life's landscape (what you've done, where you've been etc.), both figuratively and literally. Ask God to show you what direction to take – asking what, where, when and with who that your obedience or trust want cause you to interfere with His plans or perfect will.

Time to SOAR (The Interactive Work)

See, Observe, Apply and Respond

This is your opportunity to walk through the scripture reading, settle in the song, meditate on the prayer, adopt the declaration and work out the practical point. Grace is understood better through experience, take a minute to record yours.

S_____

_____

_____

O_____

_____

_____

A_____

_____

_____

R_____

_____

_____

The Space of Grace

Here is where you can write more notes, doodle or draw, drop a tear or tag a friend. You can even add a new thing about where you want grace to be seen.

Day 15

Scripture: "So I prophesied as He commanded me, and breath came into them, and they came to life and stood up on their feet an exceedingly great army." – Ezekiel 37:10 AMP

Song: Grave Digger/ Dig It Out – Psalmist Raine

Prayer: God give me the words to resuscitate the things that I've caused to die because of my speech or limited beliefs. Blow on and in them that they will come to life with strength and power. As they come up, let me manage them well and connect them piece and part one by one. Nothing will be left on the ground or in the dirt that pertains to me. Amen

Declaration: There is life in my lungs, and I command the dead things to arise, live and thrive in my life according to His will for me.

Practical Point: Speak life to your dreams and vision – past, present and future – that are unfulfilled.

Time to SOAR (The Interactive Work)

See, Observe, Apply and Respond

This is your opportunity to walk through the scripture reading, settle in the song, meditate on the prayer, adopt the declaration and work out the practical point. Grace is understood better through experience, take a minute to record yours.

S_____

_____

_____

O_____

_____

_____

A_____

_____

_____

R_____

_____

_____

The Space of Grace

Here is where you can write more notes, doodle or draw, drop a tear or tag a friend. You can even add a new thing about where you want grace to be seen.

Day 16

Scripture: Some Pharisees from the crowd told him, Teacher, get your disciples under control. But he said, if they kept quiet, the stones would do it for them, shouting praise." Luke 19:39-40 MSG

Song: So, Will I – Cross Worship ft Osby Berry

Prayer: God, I pray you never have to wait to hear my voice. I will sing praises and worship you without inhibition. May the rock or the raven, the wind nor the rain never be louder than me. Amen

Declaration: It won't be hard for heaven to notice me.

Practical Point: Identify the different ways to worship and try them out today. Not sure what that looks like, huh? Some of it has become so routine or habitual in nature it doesn't even seem different. Here are a few ways, that may even be out of the box for some:
1. Study the Word and search out new revelation and understanding.
2. Using music (listening to, singing or playing it, even dancing). David danced before the Lord, so can we.
3. Changing your posture as you pray. Adjust the way you approach the throne.
4. By serving others, according to Hebrews 13:2
5. Seek Him in everything you see, let the lens of life find God in it all (even the not so pretty stuff).

Time to SOAR (The Interactive Work)
See, Observe, Apply and Respond

This is your opportunity to walk through the scripture reading, settle in the song, meditate on the prayer, adopt the declaration and work out the practical point. Grace is understood better through experience, take a minute to record yours.

S_____

_____

_____

O_____

_____

_____

A_____

_____

_____

R_____

_____

_____

The Space of Grace

Here is where you can write more notes, doodle or draw, drop a tear or tag a friend. You can even add a new thing about where you want grace to be seen.

Day 17

Scripture: "Then Mary took a pound of very costly oil of spikenard, anointed the feet of Jesus, and wiped His feet with her hair. And the house was filled with the fragrance of the oil." - John 12:3 NKJV

Song: Like Oil – We Will Worship

Prayer: Lord all that have I pour out to you, may my worship wash over your feet along with my tears. Whether they are formed from test and trial or from a triumphant victory, may they be received with the purpose intended. May the songs of my heart saturate your seat and cause you to come look after me. May the sound of my voice be a sweet smell to you and even after I'm done, there is a beautiful residue. Amen

Declaration: I won't waste the oil on my life, yet I will pour out before Him all that I have.

Practical Point: Intentionally set your mind and mouth to worship God all day today. Set your playlist to where you can walk and worship, work and worship, rest and worship.

Time to SOAR (The Interactive Work)

See, Observe, Apply and Respond

This is your opportunity to walk through the scripture reading, settle in the song, meditate on the prayer, adopt the declaration and work out the practical point. Grace is understood better through experience, take a minute to record yours.

S_____

_____

_____

O_____

_____

_____

A_____

_____

_____

R_____

_____

_____

The Space of Grace

Here is where you can write more notes, doodle or draw, drop a tear or tag a friend. You can even add a new thing about where you want grace to be seen.

Day 18

Scripture: "Behold, I am going to do something new, now it will spring up; will you not be aware of it? I will even make a roadway in the wilderness, rivers in the desert." – Isaiah 43:18 NASB

Song: Waymaker – Sinach

Prayer: Dear Father, I thank you for caring enough to give me grace to believe and faith to cling to. Because I can put my trust in the fact that you will come through, I am no longer trapped by time but kept by your promises that it will come to pass. For being that kind of God, I say thank you and give you praise. Amen

Declaration: He has, He is, and He will make a way for me.

Practical Point: Take a minute and tell someone about what God has done…. It will be your reminder.

Time to SOAR (The Interactive Work)

See, Observe, Apply and Respond

This is your opportunity to walk through the scripture reading, settle in the song, meditate on the prayer, adopt the declaration and work out the practical point. Grace is understood better through experience, take a minute to record yours.

S_____

_____

_____

O_____

_____

_____

A_____

_____

_____

R_____

_____

_____

The Space of Grace

Here is where you can write more notes, doodle or draw, drop a tear or tag a friend. You can even add a new thing about where you want grace to be seen.

Day 19

Scripture: "And then I heard the voice of the Master: Whom shall I send? Who will go for us?" I spoke up, "I'll go. Send me!" – Isaiah 6:8 MSG

Song: Respond – Travis Greene

Prayer: God I thank you for putting out a call that I could respond to. I know that this may mean I have to do hard things by myself, but with you I am truly never alone. Let me take notice of Your tangible presence in the tough times where I gave my "yes." May I see you in the sent place, and sense you along in my journey there. Amen

Declaration: Doing it alone may be difficult, but I'll do it!

Practical Point: Look back and smile, look forward and laugh. Then say to yourself God is with me.

Time to SOAR (The Interactive Work)

See, Observe, Apply and Respond

This is your opportunity to walk through the scripture reading, settle in the song, meditate on the prayer, adopt the declaration and work out the practical point. Grace is understood better through experience, take a minute to record yours.

S_____

_____

_____

O_____

_____

_____

A_____

_____

_____

R_____

_____

_____

The Space of Grace

Here is where you can write more notes, doodle or draw, drop a tear or tag a friend. You can even add a new thing about where you want grace to be seen.

Day 20

Scripture: "With all prayer and petition pray [with specific requests] at all times [on every occasion and in every season] in the Spirit, and with this in view, stay alert with all perseverance and petition [interceding in prayer] for all God's people." - Ephesians 6:18 – AMP

Song: Song of Intercession - William McDowell

Prayer: As I lift my petitions to You, I also place every (person, place or thing) before you. That what they have need of, you will be. I pray that my prayers will activate heaven to respond on their behalf. As I bear up my brother/sister I ask that you remember us all. My faith fuels this prayer and fosters the expectation of these things to be made complete. I praise You now for your promises are yes and amen concerning us. Amen

Declaration: I will be the change I want to see in others.

Practical Point: Ask someone or two or three (smile) how can you pray for them and do it right then and continue as the Lord will allow.

Time to SOAR (The Interactive Work)

See, Observe, Apply and Respond

This is your opportunity to walk through the scripture reading, settle in the song, meditate on the prayer, adopt the declaration and work out the practical point. Grace is understood better through experience, take a minute to record yours.

S_____

_____

_____

O_____

_____

_____

A_____

_____

_____

R_____

_____

_____

The Space of Grace

Here is where you can write more notes, doodle or draw, drop a tear or tag a friend. You can even add a new thing about where you want grace to be seen.

Day 21

Scripture: "Father, if you are willing, please take this cup of suffering from me. Yet I want your will to be done, not mine." Then an angel from heaven appeared and strengthened him." – Luke 22:42-43 NLT

Song: Withholding Nothing Medley – William McDowell

Prayer: God may I give over everything beyond me, relinquishing my wanting to be in control and causing delay in my destiny. May I see Your face in my sacrifice and find assurance in the fact that my obedience gives me access to You. Amen

Declaration: In all things I'll give God everything.

Practical Point: Draw up a list of places or things that are comfortable, but you feel God wants you to surrender for him.

Time to SOAR (The Interactive Work)

See, Observe, Apply and Respond

This is your opportunity to walk through the scripture reading, settle in the song, meditate on the prayer, adopt the declaration and work out the practical point. Grace is understood better through experience, take a minute to record yours.

S_____

_____

_____

O_____

_____

_____

A_____

_____

_____

R_____

_____

_____

The Space of Grace

Here is where you can write more notes, doodle or draw, drop a tear or tag a friend. You can even add a new thing about where you want grace to be seen.

Day 22

Scripture: "There's more to come: We continue to shout praise even when we are hemmed in troubles, because we know ow troubles can develop passionate patience in us." – Romans 5:3 MSG

Song: I'm Alive – Rich Tolbert, Jr.

Prayer: God, I thank you for using each test to temper me in my faith, that I may be sustained and produce something of substance in the earth. I thank you for not ending my existence when you had every right, but giving me yet another chance to maximize my capacity based on the experiences you are using to cultivate me. I thank you for the beating, the pressing and the crushing. I've been through it and yet I am still alive, it's no mistake. Amen

Declaration: There's more and I will live to see it and be better because of it.

Practical Point: Look in the mirror every time you pass one and say to yourself "_____, (insert your name) there is more – so go after it."

Time to SOAR (The Interactive Work)

See, Observe, Apply and Respond

This is your opportunity to walk through the scripture reading, settle in the song, meditate on the prayer, adopt the declaration and work out the practical point. Grace is understood better through experience, take a minute to record yours.

S_____

_____

_____

O_____

_____

_____

A_____

_____

_____

R_____

_____

_____

The Space of Grace

Here is where you can write more notes, doodle or draw, drop a tear or tag a friend. You can even add a new thing about where you want grace to be seen.

Day 23

Scripture: "There is a season (a time appointed) for everything and a time for every delight and event or purpose under heaven." – Ecclesiastes 3:1 AMP

Song: You Make All Things Beautiful – Victor Thompson

Prayer: May I always show appreciation for the time you take with me. For the potter's wheel, and the repositioning that allows repairs to be made. God help me to see what is, recall what was and celebrate what will be. In time it all will be what heaven has declared and for that I say thank you. Amen

Declaration: Every part of me was beautiful and it's blossoming before my very eyes.

Practical Point: Stand in the mirror and simply look at yourself. Take a minute (60 seconds) to speak well of what is or is being made beautiful in the eyes of the Lord as you grow, heal and learn.

Time to SOAR (The Interactive Work)

See, Observe, Apply and Respond

This is your opportunity to walk through the scripture reading, settle in the song, meditate on the prayer, adopt the declaration and work out the practical point. Grace is understood better through experience, take a minute to record yours.

S_____

_____

_____

O_____

_____

_____

A_____

_____

_____

R_____

_____

_____

The Space of Grace

Here is where you can write more notes, doodle or draw, drop a tear or tag a friend. You can even add a new thing about where you want grace to be seen.

Day 24

Scripture: "So shall they fear the name of the Lord from the west, And His glory from the rising of the sun; When the enemy comes in like a flood, The Spirit of the Lord will lift up a standard against him." - Isaiah 59:19 NKJV

Song: Surrounded by Michael W. Smith

Prayer: God, I thank you that I will not be overtaken by the enemy, even the one called the "inner me." All matters and mindsets are subject to You and your authority. So, when overwhelm tries to overtake me, may my praise be like those who caused the Jericho walls to fall. You have raised a standard and I see it working for me. I rest in knowing heaven is at war on my behalf. Amen

Declaration: Heaven is at war for me and I'm going to see a victory!

Practical Point: Create a playlist with songs of praise, that can encourage you in the fight. Share it with someone.

Time to SOAR (The Interactive Work)

See, Observe, Apply and Respond

This is your opportunity to walk through the scripture reading, settle in the song, meditate on the prayer, adopt the declaration and work out the practical point. Grace is understood better through experience, take a minute to record yours.

S_____

_____

_____

O_____

_____

_____

A_____

_____

_____

R_____

_____

_____

The Space of Grace

Here is where you can write more notes, doodle or draw, drop a tear or tag a friend. You can even add a new thing about where you want grace to be seen.

Day 25

Scripture: "Thanks be to God, who gives us this victory through our Lord Jesus Christ!" - 1 Corinthians 15:57 CEB

Song: Never Lost by All Nations Atlanta ft. Chandler Moore & Benita Jones

Prayer: Dear God, I thank you, that no matter what I face it is never outside of your ability to conquer that thing. May my heart be encouraged, and my mind made at ease by knowing that in you I win. Let patience have her perfect work even while I wait for the enemy to wave his white flag. Amen

Declaration: I am victorious even when my vision gets cloudy, God still stands strong for me.

Practical Point: Make two lists 1) battles you've won and 2) battles you are facing. Use the first list as a reminder that despite the time you may have to face, God has and will never lose a battle fought on our behalf.

Time to SOAR (The Interactive Work)

See, Observe, Apply and Respond

This is your opportunity to walk through the scripture reading, settle in the song, meditate on the prayer, adopt the declaration and work out the practical point. Grace is understood better through experience, take a minute to record yours.

S_____

_____

_____

O_____

_____

_____

A_____

_____

_____

R_____

_____

_____

The Space of Grace

Here is where you can write more notes, doodle or draw, drop a tear or tag a friend. You can even add a new thing about where you want grace to be seen.

Day 26

Scripture: "God destined us to be his adopted children through Jesus Christ because of his love. This was according to his goodwill and plan. We have been ransomed through his Son's blood, and we have forgiveness for our failures based on his overflowing grace, which he poured over us with wisdom and understanding. We have also received an inheritance in Christ. We were destined by the plan of God, who accomplishes everything according to his design." - Ephesians 1:5, 7-8, 11 CEB

Song: Who You Say I Am by Hillsong Worship

Prayer: God the world wants me to believe I don't belong because I live and look differently. I thank you that when all have forsaken me you have called me your own. Not only is my identity made new, but I also have now inherited something the world couldn't ever give me, eternal life. Thank you for the adoption, bringing me into a forever family. Amen

Declaration: I don't have to battle with my identity, I know Who and whose I am. I am a child of God!

Practical Point: Look up what it means to be adopted and the rights and privileges that come along with being chosen. Thank God for each thing given to you.

Time to SOAR (The Interactive Work)

See, Observe, Apply and Respond

This is your opportunity to walk through the scripture reading, settle in the song, meditate on the prayer, adopt the declaration and work out the practical point. Grace is understood better through experience, take a minute to record yours.

S_____

_____

_____

O_____

_____

_____

A_____

_____

_____

R_____

_____

_____

The Space of Grace

Here is where you can write more notes, doodle or draw, drop a tear or tag a friend. You can even add a new thing about where you want grace to be seen.

Day 27

Scripture: "We saw it, we heard it, and now we're telling you so you can experience it along with us, this experience of communion with the Father and his Son, Jesus Christ. Our motive for writing is simply this: We want you to enjoy this, too. Your joy will double our joy!" - 1 John 1:3-4 MSG

Song: Evidence by Elevation Worship

Prayer: Dear God, I thank you for making my life your witness and evidence. May I always prove you are present, demonstrate your love and encapsulate your grace toward every person I encounter. I pray that how I live will always lead them to look for you. Amen

Declaration: I am His evidence, going place to place to demonstrate his love for us.

Practical Point: Share with someone your first encounter with Christ and what God has done since then.

Time to SOAR (The Interactive Work)

See, Observe, Apply and Respond

This is your opportunity to walk through the scripture reading, settle in the song, meditate on the prayer, adopt the declaration and work out the practical point. Grace is understood better through experience, take a minute to record yours.

S_____

_____

_____

O_____

_____

_____

A_____

_____

_____

R_____

_____

_____

The Space of Grace

Here is where you can write more notes, doodle or draw, drop a tear or tag a friend. You can even add a new thing about where you want grace to be seen.

Day 28

Scripture: "The sheep that are My own hear My voice and listen to ME; I know them, and they follow Me." – John 10:27 AMP

Song: Calling My Name by Hezekiah Walker

Prayer: Dear God my shepherd and father, thank you for caring enough to know the plans you had for me and where I would go away from them. Thank you for never giving up on me and coming after me even when I tried to lose you. Master, I thank you for my ability to hear, that even when I am in the lowest and darkest place when you call me, I can hear you clearly. Amen

Declaration: I am the one He left the ninety-nine for, calling my name every time I get/got lost.

Practical Point: Write out at least two times where you know you turned and left from what was right but heard God calling you back and searching to find you. Now thank Him for caring that much!

Time to SOAR (The Interactive Work)

See, Observe, Apply and Respond

This is your opportunity to walk through the scripture reading, settle in the song, meditate on the prayer, adopt the declaration and work out the practical point. Grace is understood better through experience, take a minute to record yours.

S_____

_____

_____

O_____

_____

_____

A_____

_____

_____

R_____

_____

_____

The Space of Grace

Here is where you can write more notes, doodle or draw, drop a tear or tag a friend. You can even add a new thing about where you want grace to be seen.

Day 29

Scripture: "Don't be anxious about anything; rather, bring up all of your requests to God in your prayers and petitions, along with giving thanks." Philippians 4:6 CEB

Song: Thank You by Richard Smallwood

Prayer: God you said that we should enter your gates thanksgiving, I am here before the throne and mercy seat simply to say thank you. Thank you for preserving my life, changing my name and giving me a second chance. Father, for everything that I have taken for granted I repent and return like the leper who was healed to say thank you. You didn't have to, but you did, and you did it for me the o' wretched man that I am. I count it all joy and from the bottom of my heart and depth of my soul. I say thank you Lord again and again. Amen

Declaration: I can't thank you enough, but I'll try today and forever more.

Practical Point: Name some specifics things that you want to thank God for past, present and (in hope)

Time to SOAR (The Interactive Work)

See, Observe, Apply and Respond

This is your opportunity to walk through the scripture reading, settle in the song, meditate on the prayer, adopt the declaration and work out the practical point. Grace is understood better through experience, take a minute to record yours.

S_____

_____

_____

O_____

_____

_____

A_____

_____

_____

R_____

_____

_____

The Space of Grace

Here is where you can write more notes, doodle or draw, drop a tear or tag a friend. You can even add a new thing about where you want grace to be seen.

Day 30

Scripture: "Great peace have they who love Your law; nothing shall offend them or make them stumble." – Psalm 119:165 AMPC

Song: In the Name of Jesus by Israel Haughton ft. Doe

Prayer: Lord, let me rest in the fact that you fight for me. My teeth don't have to be set on edge and my hands ready to war. You have taught me when and how to engage. Just because I am called to a battle doesn't mean I am required to respond. Help me be slow to anger and to speak, I want to be quick to listen and hear for your instructions. Make me aware of what's for me and not, that I won't exert energy in or on things that are above me because even then they are at your feet. I trust you to take care of it all. What concerns me, concerns you and you will vindicate me. Amen

Declaration: Heaven fights for me, I won't fall or fail.

Practical Point: Choose to always have the right response, knowing the battle belongs to the Lord.

Time to SOAR (The Interactive Work)

See, Observe, Apply and Respond

This is your opportunity to walk through the scripture reading, settle in the song, meditate on the prayer, adopt the declaration and work out the practical point. Grace is understood better through experience, take a minute to record yours.

S_____

_____

_____

O_____

_____

_____

A_____

_____

_____

R_____

_____

_____

The Space of Grace

Here is where you can write more notes, doodle or draw, drop a tear or tag a friend. You can even add a new thing about where you want grace to be seen.

Day 31

Scripture: "Though He slay me, yet will I trust in Him: but I will maintain mine own ways before Him. He also shall be my salvation: for a hypocrite shall not come before Him." Job 13:15-16 KJV

Song: Gratitude by Brandon Lake

Prayer: Dear God when I have nothing left, I will have my truth and testimony. Words may escape me during my tears of my laughter, but I will always have a hallelujah to offer You. I may be groaning with grief, but I will still lift a sound unto heaven. My response is even when it's not good, you still are and that is enough. I say hallelujah in hiding and exposed. You are worthy of all praise and reverence despite any and every circumstance allowed to enter my life. May it be used as an enhancement to make me better on your behalf. Amen

Declaration: Even in this I say thank You.

Practical Point: Before and after everything you do today, tell God thank you and mean it.

Time to SOAR (The Interactive Work)

See, Observe, Apply and Respond

This is your opportunity to walk through the scripture reading, settle in the song, meditate on the prayer, adopt the declaration and work out the practical point. Grace is understood better through experience, take a minute to record yours.

S_____

_____

_____

O_____

_____

_____

A_____

_____

_____

R_____

_____

_____

The Space of Grace

Here is where you can write more notes, doodle or draw, drop a tear or tag a friend. You can even add a new thing about where you want grace to be seen.

About the Author

Trish Robinson is a wife, mother, sister, daughter, and a friend. She is also a mentor, coach, pastor and creative conversationalist. Known to those around her as the Loud Leader, even when she is quiet, she has a lot to say. Trish has accepted her identity and coined it as being an agitating adjutant, the one who will irritate and assist you all at the same time. This perspective of who she was called to be was shaped by Proverbs 27:17 (AMP), where it reads "As iron sharpens iron, so one man sharpens (and influences) another (through discussion)." When she introduces herself, she simply tells people I am here to push and support you to do one of two things – either be moved into action or into an exit, either way she'll get you moving and that's the goal.

She was born in Cleveland, Ohio and raised between there and Birmingham, Alabama. Her helping heart was shaped by the lives of two great givers. Trish says she received a "double portion" of compassion for others from her mother and father who lived a life of showing up for others. Life was not always great, but if you ask her now even what was bad was still good. The challenges endured through her 44 years of living have helped to cultivate who she is and even who she's becoming. The saying hindsight is 20/20 really resonates with her because as she leads, she does so through a lens of experience, education and evaluation. Her method of teaching, preaching and coaching is based on a reflective presentation and creative conversations, her auto introduction is "this is for me, for you."

Christ has always been a presence in her life, even when she or anyone else would've begged to differ (that story will be told soon). But in February 2013, a should've been another way situation shifted how she decided to show up for Him and the people she would soon learn she was being called too. A car fire consumed everything in a moment, except her and the two bibles that were in the vehicle with her. At that point, she chose to live life and lead people the way God needed and intended for her. It took some time to come alive, but just like one of her favorite movie lines "she's here dear God, she's here." Trish served as campus pastor for 3 years at Resurrection Church alongside her husband Pastor Chris and they now copastor their own church, Road to Righteousness Ministries. Don't limit how you look for her, she may show up anywhere.

www.ingramcontent.com/pod-product-compliance
Lightning Source LLC
Chambersburg PA
CBHW020933180426
43192CB00036B/1005